CLAY REVISIONS

PLATE
CUP
VASE

CLAY REVISIONS

PLATE
CUP
VASE

by Vicki Halper
Seattle Art Museum

The exhibition *Clay Revisions: Plate, Cup, Vase* has been organized by the Seattle Art Museum and circulated by the American Federation of Arts (a merging of the Art Museum Association of America and the American Federation of Arts). Support for the publication of the catalogue came from the National Endowment for the Arts, the Contemporary Art Council and the Pacific Northwest Arts Council of the Seattle Art Museum, and the American Federation of Arts.

Catalogue coordinator: Helen Abbott
Editors: Lane Morgan and Paula Thurman
Designer: Anne Traver Graphic Design
Printed and bound in Japan by Dai Nippon Printing

LC87-082204
ISBN 0-932216-26-9

FOREWORD

The best museum exhibitions go beyond merely providing a pleasant encounter between the viewer and a group of objects. Rather they can offer new insights to the observant visitor, perhaps even a revelation, by making the old new or the new understandable. This can be achieved in a variety of ways—perhaps by combining familiar objects or images in a new context or by presenting unfamiliar objects in a traditional context. In either case, the viewer can use the traditional to make the leap to the new.

In *Clay Revisions: Plate, Cup, Vase,* curator Vicki Halper provides a historical and aesthetic context for the enjoyment and appreciation of some startling works of art. The traditional that serves as a foil for the new is our intimate knowledge of three utilitarian pottery forms—the drinking cup, the dinner plate, and the flower vase. The new context is twentieth-century painting and sculpture—nonfunctional, innovative, and exploratory. Old forms are used as subject matter for new creations in a wedding of ceramics and fine-arts traditions that is illuminating, expansive, and invigorating.

Among the many people and institutions contributing to this exhibition we wish to acknowledge particularly the following: The American Federation of Arts for its circulation of the exhibition and support of the catalogue; the National Endowment of the Arts and the Contemporary Art Council and the Pacific Northwest Arts Council of the Seattle Art Museum for additional sponsorship; Bruce Guenther, former Curator of Contemporary Art, Seattle Art Museum, and now Chief Curator at Chicago's Museum of Contemporary Art, for his unflagging support and guidance; museum staff members Liz Spitzer, Administrative Secretary, Lauren Tucker, Registrar, Helen Abbott, Publications Manager, and Paul Macapia, Photographer, for the tireless and cheerful contribution of their considerable skills. Insightful reading of the catalogue manuscript was done by William Rathbun, Rod Slemmons, Suzanne Kotz, Bonnie Pitman-Gelles, and Garth Clark. Although the responsibility for the text is finally the author's, their comments and encouragement were invaluable.

Finally we thank the lenders to the exhibition: artists, institutions, private collectors, and galleries—especially Sissy Thomas, Greenberg Gallery, St. Louis. Their credit lines in the exhibition checklist are only a small indication of their contribution to the exhibition, their trust in permitting the travel of fragile objects, and their wonderful willingness to attend to the numbing details of a long tour.

Jay Gates
Director

In *Clay Revisions*, twenty-six contemporary artists working in clay
take a new look at three traditional
vessel forms: the plate, the cup,
and the vase. Their vision is unique in one particular way—the function of these vessels is not considered. In the past, despite all varia-
tions in Western ceramic styles, from English slipware to French
rococo, utilitarian considerations have been at least a minor limitation
for ceramists, especially in those forms that are containers (bowls,
cups, vases). For the artists in this exhibition the vessel format is
adopted for many purposes—for sheer love, for dismissal, for metaphor, for comment, for play, for structure—but not for use.

These artists are experimenters and humorists, iconoclasts, gluttons
for ideas, materials, and variety. They are flouting two institutions:
the fine arts world, in which clay has long been considered a lesser
medium, and ceramic purists who believe in the sanctity of the functional vessel.

The potter's dismissal of function as a governing premise in the
construction of vessels is analogous to the painter's and sculptor's
abandonment of realism early in the twentieth century. In each case

industrialism and technology left their mark: photography created cheap perfect images and mass factory production created cheap perfect forms. This allowed for a separation between traditional craftsmanship and the expression of ideas and feelings in both ceramics and the fine arts.

The separation occurred first in the fields of painting and sculpture with the post-impressionist rejection of realism. It affected not only the depiction of people in art but also of objects, for if Picasso's women no longer had to have symmetrical features and translucent skin, his still-life vessels no longer had to maintain the illusion of holding liquids. After 1912 many sculptors took common household objects as subject matter rather than "the selective and tasteful imitation of living forms" (Elsen 1974, 52). These objects were transformed according to the artists' personal styles and beliefs: Picasso's construction *Guitar* (1912) released the instrument from its utility as music maker and divorced it from all motives ulterior to its service as an art object. That same year Umberto Boccioni sculpted *Development of a Bottle in Space* (fig. 1), a vision of the vessel as a fluid form, its interior no longer fully enclosed, its solid planes swirling into space. Five years later Constantin Brancusi began a series of large wooden cups—simplified solid forms, displacing space rather than embracing it (fig. 2). According to Sidney Geist in *Brancusi* (1968), "*Cup* is a modest creation modeled upon a commonplace artifact.... After the *head as object*, and the *torso as object*, *Cup* is the *object as object*" (quoted Elsen 1974, 56). The vessel had become a form for contemplation rather than an item to use.

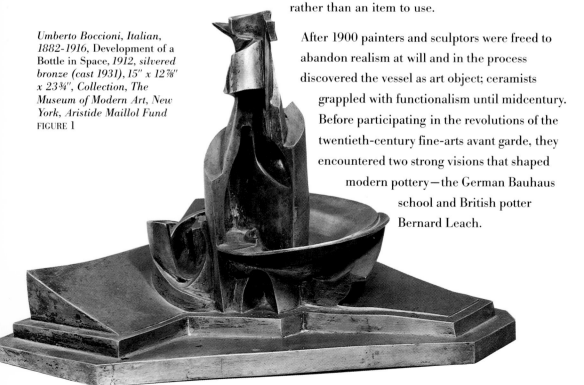

Umberto Boccioni, Italian, 1882-1916, Development of a Bottle in Space, 1912, silvered bronze (cast 1931), 15″ x 12⅞″ x 23¾″, Collection, The Museum of Modern Art, New York, Aristide Maillol Fund
FIGURE 1

After 1900 painters and sculptors were freed to abandon realism at will and in the process discovered the vessel as art object; ceramists grappled with functionalism until midcentury. Before participating in the revolutions of the twentieth-century fine-arts avant garde, they encountered two strong visions that shaped modern pottery—the German Bauhaus school and British potter Bernard Leach.

They were purists on opposite ends of the ceramic scale: the cool, controlled purists of Bauhaus industrial design and the warm, soft purists of Leach's humble folk artist-potter. Like purists in general, they illuminated the field by their intensity of focus, clarity of vision, and bold dicta: "less is more," "form follows function," "Beauty and Humility border on each other." Both the Bauhaus and Leach agreed with William Morris's dismissal of the elaborate forms of European ceramics, the "repulsively hideous" Sevres and the "most barbarous" Meissen. Leach found inspiration in the Japanese tradition of the artist-potter, and reasserted those characteristics of clay—roughness, accident, spontaneity—that were least like the values treasured in the European porcelain tradition. In addition to this disdain for flamboyance, both camps also devalued artistic individuality and self-expression and saw utility and simplicity as moral as well as aesthetic goals—means to transform a chaotic world.

Constantin Brancusi, French, 1876-1957, Cup, *1917, wood, collection of Musée National d'Art Moderne, Centre National d'Art et de Cultúre Georges Pompidou*
FIGURE 2

These concerns with function, simplicity, and anonymity isolated the potter from the fine arts world. Moreover the revolutionary painters and sculptors of the early century (Picasso, Boccioni, Brancusi) did not include clay as a medium in their wide-ranging explorations of the vessel. This is due, at least in part, to the physical nature of the material, which possesses great crushing strength but no tensile strength. It is a material of mass, to be carved or modeled, and early twentieth-century sculptors were exploring light and space through use of planar, linear, as well as transparent and reflective materials. Clay, although fluid, is opaque, and cannot become either linear or transparent, except under conditions of extreme fragility or minute scale. Moreover, it was difficult to use in assemblage sculpture until the later development of strong adhesives that would allow clay to be combined with other media outside the kiln.

In the 1950s, however, changes in the fine-arts world made an intrinsic quality of clay other than mass—its responsiveness to the immediate touch of the artist—of primary artistic value.

Peter Voulkos was the first artist to synthesize the influences of the crafts world and the fine-arts world. Between 1952 and 1953 Voulkos, both painter and production potter, had a series of intimate meetings with some of the most influential members of both groups: on an American tour, Leach and his famous Japanese collaborator, Shoji Hamada, visited Voulkos in Montana; Marguerite Wildenhain, Bauhaus emigre potter, spent five weeks at Voulkos's studio; Voulkos met Josef Albers, another Bauhaus emigre, at Black Mountain College in North Carolina, as well as musician John Cage, dancer Merce Cunningham, and artist Robert Rauschenberg. On a visit to New York City following his North Carolina workshop, Voulkos met both Franz Kline and Willem de Kooning and absorbed the electric atmosphere generated in the art world by the advent of abstract expressionist painting.

Voulkos shared with Leach and Hamada the belief that pots, like all other forms of art, are human expressions, and that accident and immediacy are to be accepted as elements in the ceramic process. Voulkos would, however, abandon their insistence on the humility of the artist and their caution against reveling in the accidental. Voulkos shared with Wildenhain an absolute control over the clay medium, but would soon turn away from the classicism and functionalism of her forms. Above all, Voulkos found in the artists of the New York school a vigor and dynamism congenial to his spirit and an approach to surface that would transform his own work into the clay equivalent of abstract expressionist painting.

For artists in the New York school, particularly de Kooning, Kline, Jackson Pollock, and Robert Motherwell, the canvas was an arena for action. The artist, a proud and lonely figure, faced the canvas courageously and left a record of the encounter in bold marks and strokes particular to him. Voulkos had in clay a perfect medium for such encounters; as a recorder of gesture, there is no material more responsive. It can be poked, pulled, cut, and torn; it can record the form of any object pressed to its surface; it can hold the most delicate or brutal of lines and the most vigorous erasures. Rose Slivka, in her landmark essay, "The New Ceramic Presence," noted how "the potter manipulates the clay itself as if it were paint—he slashes, drips, scrubs down or builds up for expressive forms and textures" (*Craft Horizons*, 1961, 4:30-37).

The clay skin became a dimensional canvas, leading to a confusion of genres: Is this painting or sculpture? Sculpture or pottery? Pottery or painting? A similar confusion was intrinsic to cubist collage and assemblage sculpture, as well as to cubist paintings, in which subjects were treated sculpturally, from all sides. The confusion of genres is embraced by many of the artists in this exhibition as the combined heritage of twentieth-century modernism and the ancient ceramic tradition of painted dimensional forms.

Slivka's article heralded a split in the American clay world. The traditionalist camp's reaction was signified by Wildenhain's cancellation of her subscription to *Craft Horizon* magazine after its publication of "The New Ceramic Presence." The avant-garde camp included not only those who joined Voulkos in creating expressionist ceramics, but those who would thereafter become engaged with ideas current in the fine arts.

The community sympathetic to Voulkos responded not only to his overwhelming presence but to the romantic expressionism that informed his work. Robert Arneson, for example, was a well-schooled functional potter in northern California when he turned his attention toward the revolutionary work of Voulkos. After struggling with his own "pottery-skill mentality," he abandoned traditional ceramics in 1960, adopting an abstract style similar to Voulkos's. In 1963, under pressure to present himself independently, and after reflecting on his heritage as a ceramist, he created a toilet, "the ultimate ceramics in western culture," for an exhibition that included the work of Voulkos, among others. Even Arneson found his own creation shocking (Benezra 1985, 17-23).

The toilet was a reaction to the ceramics of Peter Voulkos as well as to the Bay Area abstract expressionist painting of Clyfford Still and Mark Rothko, who taught there in the 1940s. It was part of a climate of reaction that involved artists on both coasts—pop artists (Claes Oldenberg, Roy Lichtenstein (fig. 3), and Jasper Johns, for example) in the East, and funk artists (William T. Wiley and Roy de Forest, for example) in the West. While both groups used objects as subject matter for their art, funk had a raw edge—a crudeness of execution and an outrageous sexual or scatalogical suggestiveness—that was foreign to the cooler and more subtle pop art.

On the West Coast, clay was an important medium for the midcentury return of the object as subject matter for avant-garde art. Cubist painters had been interested in objects mainly for spatial manipulations that undermined the sense of mass, but Arneson, like pop sculptors, was interested in objects as powerful things-in-themselves that could be treated as sculptural mass, a treatment highly compatible with the clay medium. Thus Arneson, like Voulkos, used clay for the exploration of ideas and problems external to the traditional potter's world, in an atmosphere congenial to both his artistic interests and to his chosen medium.

Clay Revisions: Plate, Cup, Vase charts more recent encounters between the world of the painter and the sculptor. Not all the artists represented in this exhibition use clay with the fluid bravado that unites Voulkos and Arneson. Other artistic concerns call for differing treatments of the medium—a constructivist rigidity or a conceptual spareness, for example. But all of the artists have chosen, at least in the works presented here, to address two traditions that did not meet head on until recently—the tradition of the functional craftsman and the heritage of twentieth-century modernism.

Roy Lichtenstein, American, b. 1923, Ceramic Sculpture #9, 1965, glazed ceramic, 10" x 8½" x 8½", collection of Mr. and Mrs. Bagley Wright
FIGURE 3

PLATE

 he plate is the potter's canvas, the draftsman's blank page. It is the least specific and the least articulated of the traditional utilitarian forms, and the one most easily adapted for purely aesthetic aims. The plate gives us the simplest view of ceramics—of surface alone distinct from sculptural form—and allows us to focus on those aspects of the medium that differentiate it from painting. These are specifically the nonrectangular format of the plate, and the special characteristics of clay that allow it to be modeled and carved as well as painted and glazed.

Spiral pattern on a wheel-thrown contemporary plate.
FIGURE 4

CIRCLE, SPIRAL, STAR

Except for a short period in the Renaissance when the tondo frame was in vogue, painters generally have used a rectangular format. The ninety-degree angle is natural to wood, which can be curved only with great difficulty and skill, and the rectangular format is inherently interesting, characterized by a certain dynamism, with the points of greatest tension at the corners. The disposition of the canvas as horizontal or vertical has been expressive in itself—the horizontal suggesting landscape, the vertical suggesting portrait. The ceramist's canvas is the circle, and sometimes the oval. This is because the major

Plate, *Hispano-Moresque, 16th century, glazed earthenware, 15⅝″ x 15⅝″ x 2¼″, Seattle Art Museum, Eugene Fuller Memorial Collection, 49.29*
FIGURE 5

method of shaping clay—working it on a potter's wheel—produces a circular shape. However, unlike the rectangle, the circle is a shape without inherent tensions. It has an absolute and binding center that is equally distant from all parts of the rim. The rectangle sits solidly on its horizontal base while the circle floats. The patterns natural to the surface of the plate are the gentle, endless spiral (the ridge made by the fingers on a wheel-thrown shape) (fig. 4); concentric circles, constricting toward the center (fig. 5); and the star with all lines radiating from the locus (fig. 6). The patterns natural to the surface of the canvas are the stripe and the grid, expansive as the spiral but strongly interlocking in design, and nonrestrictive as to the pattern's center.

Artists have always been concerned about the relationship of image to frame, but with the advent of abstract art, particularly the formalist works of the 1970s, this concern became an obsession for some. Many ceramists working in a circular format moved beyond a calming center or languid turning, adding off-center tensions that nevertheless acknowledged the traditional form, though not always the function, of a plate.

The most traditional plates in *Clay Revisions* are two by Arneson from his *Describing the Diameter* series (pl. 2). They are traditional because they have a broad, defined rim that acts as a frame for the image in

Plate, *French or English, style of Bernard Palissy, 19th century, glazed earthenware, 9¼" x 9¼" x 2", Seattle Art Museum, Eugene Fuller Memorial Collection, 50.53*
FIGURE 6

Robert Arneson, A Question of Measure with Colored Grid, *1980, glaze, slip, china paint, and luster on earthenware, 18¾″ x 18¾″ x 2″, collection of Robert Arneson and Sandra Shannonhouse*
PLATE 2

the center. Arneson's image, a sculpted man with multiple splayed arms and legs, is adapted from a famous Leonardo da Vinci drawing, *The Proportions of Man* (c. 1490). Arneson creates tension not so much in the figure's form, a variant of the radiating star pattern, as in its satiric content: Man, the measure of all things, is the dumpy, bearded artist himself, hands tucked casually beneath the lifted rim of the plate.

Each of Arneson's plates is a parody of another artist's style. One is a humorous tribute to Voulkos, master of ceramic holes and gashes and macho figure par excellence. On its stoneware-like surface a blowout, a hole, eliminates the artist's phallus. In another work from this series, the plate is broken, glazed, and glued back to its original shape, recalling the archaeological method of ceramist Rick Dillingham. This plate has three layers of patterning: the sculptor's relief figure, the painter's grid, and the potter's broken shards.

Patrick Siler's plate *Bow-wow* (pl. 3) also has a frame of sorts, though it is painted onto the surface rather than articulated in a traditional clay rim. This frame appears to be a circle of overlapping playing cards. They leave an irregular hexagonal peephole in the center of the plate through which we glimpse a scene of a dog chasing a car. The image suggests both rotation, in the car's spinning wheel, and strong lateral movement, in the path of dog and car across the surface.

Patrick Siler, Bow-wow, *1975, glazed stoneware, 14½″ x 14½″ x 1¼″, courtesy of the artist and Linda Farris Gallery, Seattle*
PLATE 3

The opposition of circular to lateral movement is intensified in Robert Sperry's plate (pl. 4)—an elegant abstract counterpoint to Siler's cartoonlike image. Sperry has attacked the endless rotation of the concentric circles that echo the plate's edge by a commanding lateral sweep that bisects the plate in a wide band. In another plate he also dominates the circle by taking the inherent spiral pattern of the thrown form and turning it into a maelstrom of crackling glaze. The center of this spiral is not the center of the plate, and this dislocation or eccentricity creates tension and illusionistic distortion in the planar surface.

Viola Frey uses the vertiginous spin of the spiral for a nightmare of whirling horse, face, and hand (pl. 5). The absence of a horizontal anchor is a metaphor for the absence of an emotional as well as a physical anchor—there is no solid ground. To the dislocation of space she adds both confusion of scale and arbitrary color. Is the horse a knick-knack or the reduced image of a real animal? Is the face a doll, a ghost, or a cartoon of a person?

Viola Frey, Winged Horse with Compartment, *1986, glazed whiteware, 27" x 27" x 3", courtesy of Rena Bransten Gallery, San Francisco*
PLATE 5

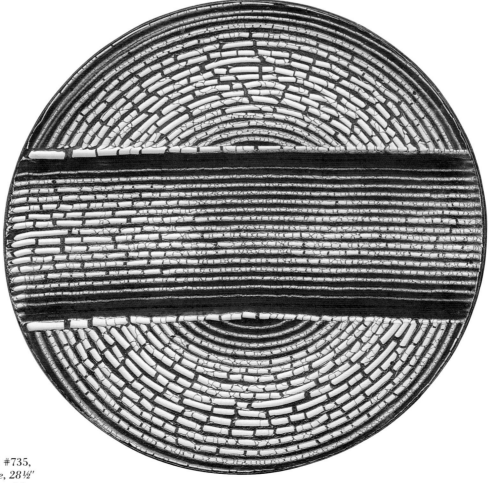

Robert Sperry, Untitled #735, *1986, slip on stoneware, 28½" x 28½" x 4½", courtesy of the artist*
PLATE 4

Jamie Walker, Double Spiral, 1986, glaze and slip on porcelain, 23" x 17" x 3", courtesy of Dorothy Weiss Gallery, San Francisco
PLATE 6

Both Jamie Walker and Jun Kaneko use an oval format for their plates (pls. 6 and 7). This compromise between the rectangle and the circle has elements of each—a clear directionality (horizontal or vertical) combined with softness of contour. Like Sperry, both artists manipulate the spiral to create depth and tension. Kaneko turns the spiral into a multicolored ribbon and unravels it from the center of the plate, or curls it diagonally, like a spring, across the surface. Walker doubles the spiral and squeezes two circular shapes formed by the tightest coils side by side onto his oval plate. The doubling of image leads to a double focus and the two orange spirals press against the plate's green rim, pushing and elongating the oval frame.

Jun Kaneko, Untitled Plate #403, 1987, glaze and slip on stoneware, 25" x 21" x 2½", courtesy of Klein Gallery, Chicago
PLATE 7

Three artists in *Clay Revisions*—Mike Moran, Stan Welsh, and Voulkos—consciously break the plate's rim and disrupt its circular frame. The disruption gives instant focus to the work and creates tensions through its foiling of expectations. In Moran's *Woman on a Black Horse* (pl. 8), the naked rider conquers the restrictions of weight and mass by riding out of the substantial body of the plate and into the air. In Welsh's *Mind Puzzle* (pl. 9), two shards, perhaps from an earlier broken piece, become the ears for a troubled head. In Voulkos's 1982 plate the break is like a geological fault, a crumbling at the end of a strong line carved into the plate's surface (pl. 10).

PAINTER, SCULPTOR, MIMIC

No matter how the picture plane is organized, the nature of the clay surface remains integral to the work. The artist's cuts, brushstrokes, and modelings can be said to decorate the surface of the plate only as much as oil paint can be said to decorate the surface of the canvas (Woodman, *American Ceramics*, 1982, 1:30-33). The plate as artist's tablet continues to attract even those whose sculptural work in clay has not been concerned with the vessel.

Stan Welsh, Mind Puzzle, *1986, glazed earthenware, 24″ x 26″ x 4½″, courtesy of Dorothy Weiss Gallery, San Francisco*
PLATE 9

Michael Moran, Woman on a Black Horse, *1986, glaze, slip, and miscellaneous fired materials on stoneware, 21″ x 21″ x 2½″, Seattle Art Museum, purchased with funds from the Anne Gould Hauberg Craft Fund, 87.12*
PLATE 8

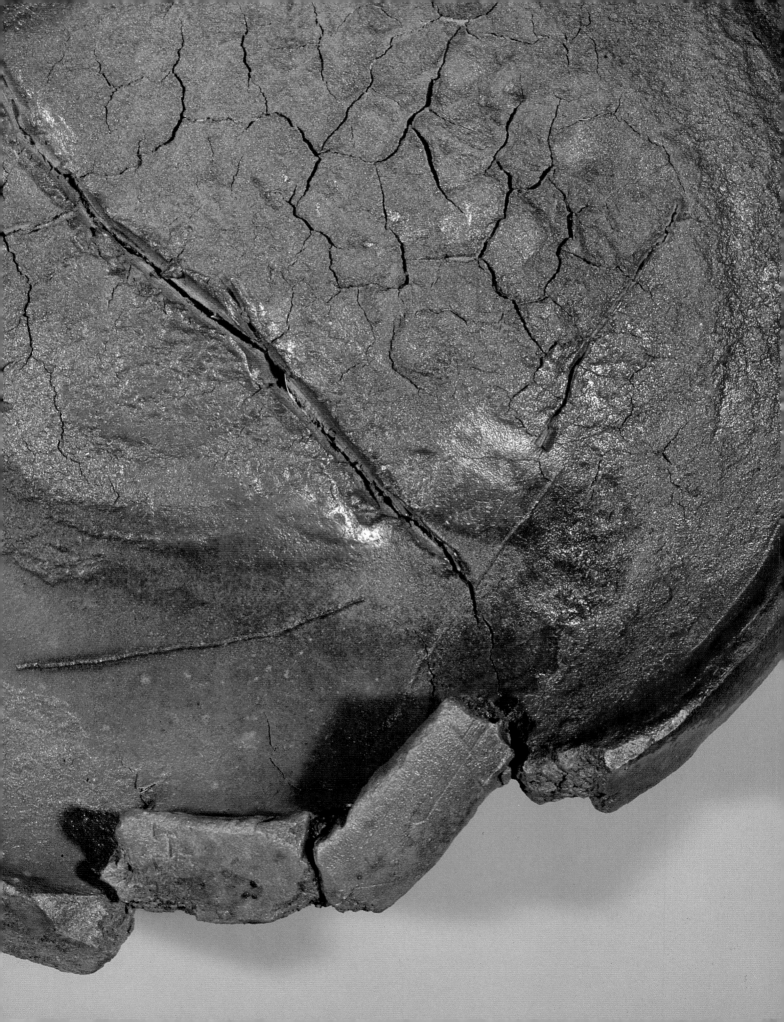

Peter Voulkos, Untitled (RB 11), *1982, stoneware, 22" x 22" x 5½", courtesy of Braunstein/Quay Gallery, San Francisco and Images Gallery, Sun Valley, Idaho*
PLATE 10

As painter alone, the artist can brush thin washes or thick impastoes of color onto the finished clay form. As sketcher, using stick rather than pen, the artist can engrave the most responsive of lines. As sculptor the artist can build up or subtract from the clay surface, layering and attaching or gouging and carving with the simplest of tools or with the hand alone.

Fine European porcelains minimized the sense of any direct modeling by hand and emphasized a sleek glazed surface for display of the most painterly aspect of the ceramic arts. The Leach revival turned attention away from polished porcelain to the surfaces created by Japanese and folk potters—rougher, less regular, more likely to bear the marks of the earth, the hand, and the fire. It is this sensibility that Voulkos applies to his own work. His plates display tension between spontaneity and control—boldness of gesture and the restraint in making marks; between the control of the circular plate shape and its seeming geological dissolution; and between the pattern of handmade marks and the pattern of the fire. In these unglazed pieces, clay speaks for itself.

Deep plate, *Portuguese, style
of Bernard Palissy, Mafra factory, c. 1900, glazed earthenware, 11⅝″ x 11⅝″ x 4½″,
Seattle Art Museum, gift of
Mrs. Alice C. Cunningham
in memory of her husband,
Ralston R. Cunningham, 75.11*
FIGURE 7

In Arneson's *Dirty Dish* series, calculated self-consciousness replaces
the abandon of Voulkos. The heritage of cubism, dada, and pop are
evident in the combination of painting and sculpture genres and in
subject matter that is common and somewhat unappealing—a leftover
meal (pl. 11). The European mannerist tradition of the seventeenth
century is also an inheritance. Allison Britton, in her introduction to
Peter Dormer's *The New Ceramics* (1986), compares the complexity
and self-consciousness of seventeenth-century mannerism to contemporary ceramics, as distinct from what she calls the classicism of
Leach. Common to mannerism and contemporary ceramics are the
disjunction of form and function, capriciousness, self-concern, and
exaggeration. In ceramics, the late sixteenth-century work of Bernard
Palissy (and his imitators) is an example (fig. 7). His plates were
ornamented with relief ceramic creatures, perhaps cast from real
lizards and frogs.

Arneson's own oval plates, ornamented with bits of food, are, like
Palissy ware, part trompe l'oeil and part whimsy. But *Dirty Dish* is

Robert Arneson, Dirty Dish, *1971, glaze and china paint on whiteware, 8½" x 20½" x 8½", Seattle Art Museum, gift of the Sidney and Anne Gerber Collection, 86.272*
PLATE 11

not really a sculpture of a dish of leftovers—it is a sculpture of a still-life painting. This imaginary painting (perhaps by Wayne Thiebaud) is of a round plate with knife and fork resting on it. The painter draws the dish as an oval, since that is how it appears in perspective. Likewise the tines of the fork are foreshortened. The painter carefully adds the shadows cast by each object, using a dark purplish hue. Arneson, in translating the painting into sculpture, models an oval plate, not a round one, and displays it at a tilted angle; the tines of his three-dimensional fork are cut off as the fork curls around the knife, foreshortening the object; shadows are painted for each solid object— food, fork, knife, dish—as well as for the painted remains of the meal depicted on the plate. Arneson's plate, utensils, and leftovers also cast their own shadows under the real lights in the gallery. His painted shadows, oval plate, and watercolor-like rendering of the glazed surface of each object are part of a contemporary dialogue between painter and sculptor.

In Arneson's *Dirty Dish* series, we are fooled into thinking a sculpture is a painting. In Richard Shaw's plates, we are fooled into thinking clay is printed paper and the glazed clay surface is a collage (pl. 12). His trompe l'oeil techniques are a quantum leap from those of earlier practitioners (e.g., the ceramics of the French Niderviller factory in the mideighteenth century, or the paintings of William Harnett in the nineteenth century), because of his sophisticated use of photographic transfer printing and his manipulation of clay and glazes to create both the textures and finishes of the objects he is imitating. In traditional trompe l'oeil ceramics there is a uniform glossiness of surface, and in painting a relative dullness of oils. Clay, because of its sculptural flexibility and the limitless possibilities of surface finishes, is a perfect mimetic medium.

Shaw's clay collages are directly related to the early twentieth-century collages of the cubists and surrealists in their incorporation of printed mass-media images that are incongruously juxtaposed. They also recall the collages of abstract expressionist painter Motherwell. Shaw as a potter, however, uses the circular format, and his printed shards float in atmospheric soup. Like other artists using plate formats, he works both to acknowledge the lip of the plate and to deny the absoluteness of the center. He does this by offsetting the circular area of the collage from the center of the plate, creating a partial crescent rim and breaking the traditional concentric pattern of image within frame.

Richard Shaw, Untitled (25 B), *1986, glaze and decals on porcelain, 20" x 20" x 1¾", courtesy of Braunstein/Quay Gallery, San Francisco*
PLATE 12

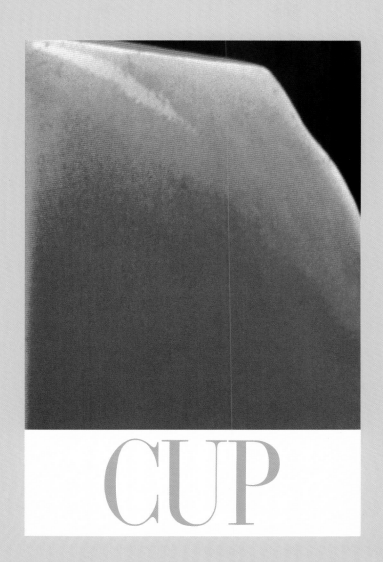

CUP

Vessels used to hold tea are among the most intimate of utilitarian objects. The drinker cradles the cup or holds its handle and brings it up to the face. Lips and tongue touch the rim of the bowl, steam bathes the face while the nose registers the scent of the brew. The cup must fulfill both aesthetic and engineering criteria: it must be sensually pleasing to both fingers and lips and must be balanced and light (fig. 8).

Teacup and saucer, *European, c. 1900, porcelain, 5¼" (diameter of saucer)*
FIGURE 8

The Japanese raku tea bowl (fig. 9) is a relatively simple affair compared to its English cousin, the teacup. The tea bowl is a hymn to the nature of clay as earth, the spontaneous spirit of the potter, and the unpredictable workings of the fire. Yet despite the rigor and gravity of the tea ceremony and the Japanese/Leach tradition of rustic-chic, the raku tea bowl is basically an irregular footed cylinder.

Tea bowl, named Tamamushi (Golden Beetle), *Japanese, Edo period, early 17th century, black raku ware, glazed earthenware, 3⅜" x 5" x 5", Seattle Art Museum, gift of Dr. Masatoshi Okochi, 52.68*
FIGURE 9

The English teacup is a complex object, reflecting perhaps its aristocratic heritage: the bowl inherited from the Chinese and Japanese, the handle added by Europeans in the mideighteenth century, and the saucer developed by the French in the late eighteenth century and adopted as late as the early nineteenth century by the English. The bowl is a hollow hemisphere meant to hold liquids; the handle, a linear coil through which light can be seen, is attached to the bowl; the cup sits on the circular plane of the saucer. The handle gives a strong asymmetry to the cup and creates an additional engineering problem—how can the fragile linear coil support and balance the weight of the full bowl, a question humorously answered by Peter Shire in his *Checkered Peach Cup* (pl. 13).

The problems of spilled liquids and scalded lips are not addressed by the artists in *Clay Revisions*. But other aspects of the traditional teacup are embraced or scrutinized. These are the intimacy, as expressed in small scale rather than physical proximity, and the architectonics of asymmetry and balance, unrelated to functional problems of containment and heft. The teacup is also a vehicle for other investigations: the relation of solid to void and line to mass as well as metaphors of empty and full and of the human body, particularly the head, as container.

Peter Shire, Checkered Peach Cup, *1977-78, colored earthenware, 4" x 8" x 3¼", collection of the artist*
PLATE 13

S C A L E

Much of the power of monumental sculpture lies in its ability to envelop one's field of vision and to thereby diminish and overwhelm the viewer. On the other hand, the power of small objects lies in their ability to narrow and concentrate the attention of the viewer. A small object can achieve this either when it is a miniature of something larger, as in Arneson's *Mountain Cup #18* (pl. 14), or by the dominating presence of its intrinsic proportions, as in Kenneth Price's geometric cups (see cover and pl. 16). It is the world itself, not the viewer, that shrinks.

For Price and Ron Nagle, who both worked with Voulkos, the turn to intimate scale and brilliant color was daring in its disregard for acceptable avant-garde behavior. It was in fact a move that acknowledged the hobbyist's brightly colored, low-fired whiteware, reliant on industry for glaze and firing technology. In these aspects, Price and Nagle were like the northern California funk school surrounding Arneson. But in the precision and coolness of their non-narrative constructions and in the architectonics of their forms there are recollections of European constructivism and De Stijl formalism foreign to both expressionism and funk.

The geometric works of Price and Nagle have an authoritative presence achieved through formal rather than narrative means. The cup, with its vocabulary of containment (bowl) and appendage (handle) is their structural starting point. In Nagle's work (pl. 15) the handle soon becomes a vestigial notch or lump, one of many small tensions in works that, like Japanese raku tea bowls, are refined and subtle. But unlike the rough, fluid liveliness of the raku bowl, his work is exotically colored and tightly controlled, an orchestrated discourse on the relationship of contour to painted plane.

Ron Nagle, Untitled VI/7.2.82, 1982, glaze and china paint on whiteware, 6½″ x 3¾″ x 3¾″, collection of Mr. and Mrs. William L. Nussbaum
PLATE 15

Robert Arneson, Mountain Cup #18, 1972, glaze and slip on whiteware, 4″ x 5½″ x 6¾″, collection of Robert Arneson and Sandra Shannonhouse; courtesy of Fuller Goldeen Gallery, San Francisco
PLATE 14

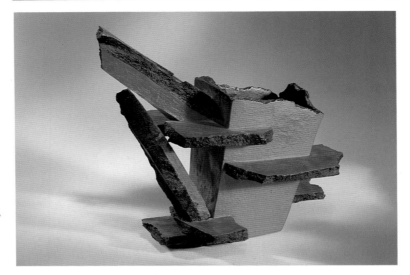

Kenneth Price, Slate Cup, *1972, acrylic on whiteware, 5 ½" x 6" x 5", collection of Edwin Janss*
PLATE 16

The handles in Price's geometric cups are more dominant and varied (cover and pl. 16). They slice and tumble from the rigid bowl, following the geometric logic of slab construction—no bulges or curves, just planes and edges: faceted geometric solids or thick torn slices of clay. Saucers are often indicated by stabilizing projections at the base of the bowl or by a separate, movable component, as distinct from the cup as the traditional plate. Each plane is differentiated from the others by color. Where the carefully cut surfaces meet, a white edge is formed by glazes retreating from the sharp angle; where thick slabs are torn, the ragged edge is differentiated from the smooth plane by color.

Arneson plays with scale. His bowl is a miniature mountain rising out of the puddled liquid in the saucer's plane (see pl. 14). Like Brancusi, he has turned the bowl of his cup into a solid. However, his cup is not Brancusi's elegant hemispherical abstraction (see fig. 2) but a solid, earthy rock dominating a glazed sea. Absurdly, a teacup handle is stuck to the side of the mountain. The clash between intimate and monumental is exaggerated by this contrast between fragility and weight. In Arneson's *Sinking Cup* (1974), the saucer becomes even more of a sea, swallowing the cup, except for one side and the protruding handle. Perhaps this is the artist's farewell to the cup, with its stolid functionalism and ties to the craft tradition, as he had said good-bye to the bottle in 1962 by capping it and stamping "No Return" on its side.

Tony Hepburn also places his cups in a geological context (pl. 17). Although his environment is abstract and severe in comparison to Arneson's, the vessel is in a similar precarious situation. A saucer should hold and stabilize a cup, not drown it or tip it dangerously on a slope. Hepburn's cup rests on one of three slanted planes, huddled against a small outcropping of ceramic slabs. The permanence of fired clay contrasts with the instability of the composition, as the carefully machined edges contrast with torn clay chunks. The combination of geology and artifice forms a landscape in which the cup is a monumental component, startling in its familiarity and disconcerting in this strange context.

Tony Hepburn, Cup Slide, *1979, glazed stoneware and porcelain, 7" x 24" x 13", collection of Laura Hepburn*
PLATE 17

Irvin Tepper, Bright Ideas, *1986, porcelain, 9¾" x 10" x 14", courtesy of Gallery Paule Anglim, San Francisco*
PLATE 18

VOID

Of the cup's functional components the bowl is the most essential. One can serve liquids without saucers and without handles, but not without the container for the brew. The uncompromising demand of the cup's function refers to something extrinsic to the object: the fluid, without which the cup is incomplete. Eliminating the functional aspect of the cup frees the artist to examine and play with the bowl. Arneson, for example, turned the bowl into a solid in *Mountain Cup #18* (see pl. 14) and floated it in a saucer of liquid, reversing the accustomed relationship of wet to dry.

Other artists concentrate on the empty space in an unfilled cup and focus our attention on the void itself by dematerializing the bowl. Irvin Tepper shaves and pierces the bowl and creates a painful fragility (pl. 18). It is light, not liquid, that fills the cup and washes through its stressed surface. His cup becomes a small universe, intensely precarious—a world that might shatter at any instant. Even without the lengthy narratives that often accompany Tepper's cups, we feel there are stories surrounding these objects.

In Tepper's cups the light leaks through the fractured bowl. In Howard Kottler's *Cup of Lite* (pl. 19), the solid surface disappears beside the intensity of the lit interior. Kottler creates a shape derived from the plaster mold used to manufacture slipcast cups. The mold is a negative from which a positive, the finished cup, is made. The negative, actually one half of the full mold, is like a cup sliced in two to fully reveal the inside of the bowl. The shell is then filled with light and the cup's skin becomes simply a frame to contain it. As Arneson reverses fluid and solid in his *Mountain Cup #18*, Kottler reverses light and dark, positive and negative.

Howard Kottler, Cup of Lite, *1973, whiteware, 5" x 7" x 3", courtesy of the artist*
PLATE 19

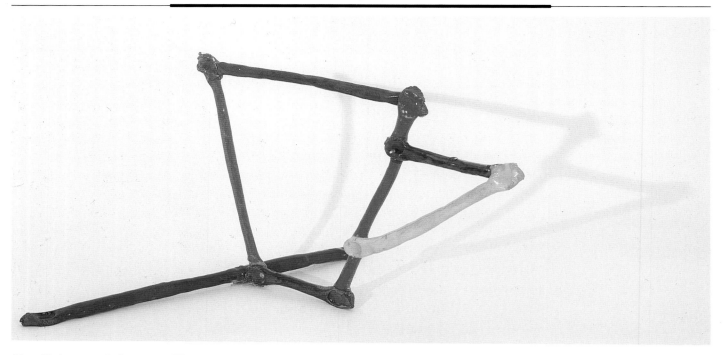

The intellectualization and dematerialization of the cup take another
leap with Mary Heilmann's *3-D Cup Drawing* (pl. 20). Her coil outline
is a hieroglyph for the letters c-u-p. She gives us a dimensional picto-
graph rather than a metaphorical or narrative object. She is not interested in what a cup means or how it is used, but only in the fact that we
recognize a sign and call it by a name. Heilmann creates this sign by
the most elemental of ceramic methods—a set of variously colored,
hand-rolled coil snakes, pressed together with flat thumb marks. These
coils are the alphabet of the potter, as meaningless as random letters
until given a sequence by the artist.

CUP AS HEAD

Drinking vessels in the shape of the human head have long been associated with inebriation, particulary British mask and satyr mugs of the
eighteenth and nineteenth centuries. These are works we can imagine
hefted in hearty, if tipsy, fellowship. On the other hand, the heads in
Tom Rippon's and Olga Bravo's cups are images of tension and strained
nervousness, neurasthenic rather than jolly. Like irritable early morning risers, these heads project a hostile unwillingness to greet the world.
Rippon's *Miss-Stress #1* (pl. 23), all slanted eyes and bared teeth, has a
finger stuck in her ear. The sweep of the arm to the head forms the handle for the cup. Olga Bravo's *Cup and Saucer* (pl. 21) has a similar
sharpness. The bowl is compressed to a narrow slit, the handle is a
pointed ear, the hair is a pattern of zig-zags, hotly colored against the
green of the face. The saucer is like a wide curved collar to the head
and, with its footed base, is also a miniature table for the cup. In other
pieces, Bravo's saucer becomes the shoulders of the figure.

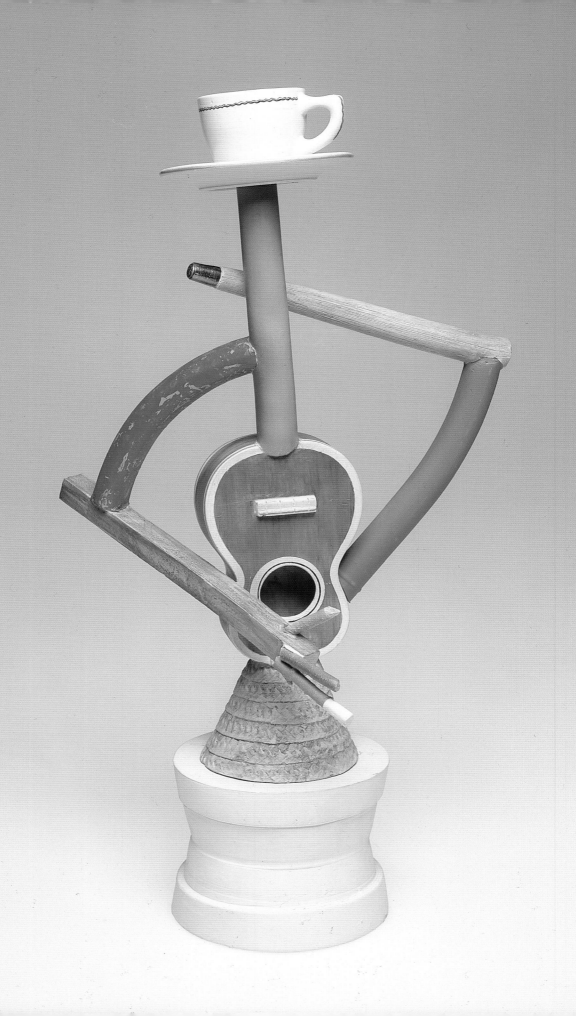

After the demanding personalities of Bravo's and Rippon's cups, the plain white cup-head in Richard Shaw's figure *Cubist Coffee Cup* (pl. 22), is startling. It arrests us by its recognizability and homeliness and by its failure to make any concessions to our usual notion of head (eyes, nose, mouth). The figure itself is assembled from clay parts that mimic other materials—twigs, scrap wood, basketry, chair legs, musical instruments—and a porcelain cup, which is simply itself. The cup functions in *Cubist Coffee Cup* just as the "real" objects do in Picasso's cubist collages and sculptures, for example, the piece of commercial sheet music in *Guitar, Sheet Music, and Wine Glass* (1912). In the artist's world of artifice and virtuosity, the mundane confuses expectations and destroys distinctions between objects that are suitable for use and objects that are suitable for art. The context—art, sculpture—defines the object.

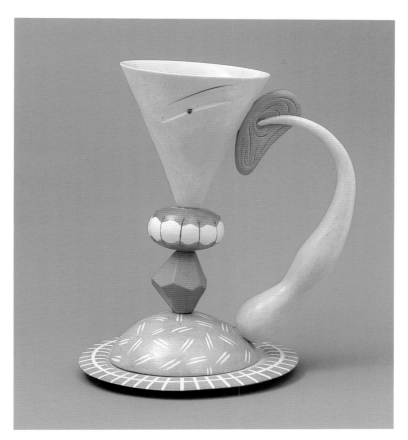

Shaw creates a figure that is both instrument and player at once by equating the body of a viol with the body of a man. He uses both Picasso's vocabulary of images (musicians, instruments, vessels) and Picasso's method of construction—additive accretion of parts rather than carving or modeling. But Shaw's figure is not essentially cubist in style—he does not dissect, flay, or flatten his subject, nor does he reverse solid and void. We see the title *Cubist Coffee Cup* and laugh, comparing this empty-headed figure to the analytic and synthetic cubist creations of Picasso.

VASE

The vase is the archetype of clay construction. It is a freestanding, hollow, vertical sleeve, which can be transformed into a decorative or utilitarian vessel or a figurative or abstract sculpture. The vessel form is intrinsic to the manner of constructing any sizable work in clay, which must generally be worked around a hollow core. This is because the medium, in its transformation from wet to dry to fired, shrinks and releases moisture and gases. Drying and firing an object without cracking or destroying it usually depends on the relative thinness and uniformity of its clay walls. Throwing on the wheel, pinching, and coil building have in common a circling of the interior.

The clay sleeve is usually called a vessel when the interior is exposed through an opening at the top, when the silhouette is relatively symmetrical, and when function is clearly implied. The clay sleeve is usually called a sculpture when the interior is unavailable or disregarded or obscured, when the silhouette of the piece changes radically with the angle of viewing, and when there is definable subject matter

Vase, British, Worcester factory, First period (1751-76), porcelain with overglaze decoration, 8⅝″ x 4⅛″ x 4⅛″, Seattle Art Museum, gift of an anonymous donor, 55.91
FIGURE 10

divorced from utility. A clear distinction between vessel and sculpture cannot always be made.

SILHOUETTE

Most of the vases in *Clay Revisions* are vessels and can be discussed in traditional terminology. In ceramics texts, the parts of the vase are illustrated by a flat black silhouette with labeled segments: lip, neck, shoulder, belly, foot. The silhouette is bilaterally symmetrical and the curves are smooth and taut. The contours of the vase are constricted or ballooned either gently or with definite articulation. The generic vase used for the illustration could be either Song dynasty or Renaissance revival in type. We imagine the silhouette refers to an elegant porcelain vessel (fig. 10).

A Voulkos vase (or "stack") differs from this image in many significant ways (pl. 24). Stoneware replaces porcelain; rough surface replaces smooth; disjunction of parts (the stacking of separate units) replaces elision of parts; lax contours replace taut ones; accident, disruption, and decay replace perfection and control; personality replaces anonymity. In the metaphorical terminology developed by Jeff Perrone in "More Sherds," (*American Ceramics*, 1986, 4:24–37), the classical diagram is an example of "centering"; the Voulkos stack is an example of "throwing."

Peter Voulkos, Untitled, 1982, stoneware, 42" x 28" x 28", collection of Mr. and Mrs. William L. Nussbaum
PLATE 24

There are more traditional vases than Voulkos's in *Clay Revisions*. A silhouette of Walker's vase would show bold, symmetrical contours and a crisp, if exaggerated, articulation of lip, belly, and foot (pl. 1). This silhouette would not, however, show his daring use of color and surface to emphasize this articulation of parts and to force attention to the inside of the broadly flared and welcoming lip.

Betty Woodman does not require that we imagine the silhouette of her pot (pl. 25). She creates it herself out of clay and hangs it on the wall behind her vase as its shadow. What the shadow emphasizes is the strength and simplicity of her form and the clarity and sureness of her articulations. It also exaggerates the weight and fluidity of the flamboyant handles and forces us to remember the important void created by that linear attachment. The shadow, like the vase, is bilaterally symmetrical. But the piece as a whole is not. The front and back of the vessel, as defined by the placement of the handles, are colored differently. There is an asymmetry of surface in contrast to symmetry of profile. Moreover, the shadow hangs to one side of the vase, creating a forceful imbalance.

There is more to Woodman's shadows than the projected contour of the vase. In *Sturdy Vase and Shadow* the shadow is the counterpoint to the vessel before it: the vessel is volumetric, but its surface decoration is flat; the shadow is flat, but its surface decoration is dimensional. The checkerboard pattern on the vase is created by strong alternating colors. The color differentiates the neck from the body (as in Walker's vase), causes the surface asymmetry between the front and back of the vase, and creates the illusion of a flattened form by obscuring the natural play of light on a convex surface. Flatness is also suggested in the use of a gridlike pattern that is most strongly identified with rectangular formats.

Woodman's shadow starts with a wheel-thrown plate marked with the spiral ridges made by the artist's hands. After removal from the wheel, the plate is thrown again, literally tossed on the floor, to elongate the circle into an oval and to emphasize the spiral ridge. The shadow is cut from this plate. Sprigged criss-crosses are added to the surface, partially obscuring the spiral. The whole shadow is given a fluid amber glaze which pools and darkens in the recesses of the surface. The single color permits light to play freely over the surface; the raised decoration creates its own shadow. Patterning on the flat shadow lends depth to the shape just as patterning on the dimensional vessel robs the vase of its rotundness.

Perrone has an additional interpretation of Woodman's shadows. He thinks of them as manifestations of the dark interior of the vessel, a revelation of the void (*The Ceramics of Betty Woodman*, 1985). The still and mysterious center of the vessel would then be manifest on the vertical shadow as the epicenter of the spiral, sitting at the heart of the image.

Kottler's vase, like Woodman's shadow, is an exposure of the interior of a vessel in a planar composition. *Portrait of a Vase* (pl. 26) is a flat image made by a conventional optical illusion: when two human profiles face each other, the void between can be read as a vase. It depends upon focus, whether one concentrates on the positive (head) or negative (vase) image. The profiles Kottler uses are his own. The artist creates the vase shape but has an ambiguous relationship to it. He has created an idea rather than an object—the vase is simply air.

SURFACE

The body of a vessel does not go from edge to edge as its silhouette implies. It is sculptural; it displaces and encircles space. Like other sculptural materials, clay has its characteristic surfaces—bronze has a patina, marble a luster, wood a grain, clay a roughness and opacity. Clay can also be given various textures, as wood can be chipped or sanded, or marble can be abraded or polished. The plasticity and impressionability of clay make the textural possibilities of its surface infinite. In the works of Voulkos and Hepburn, the possibilities of natural clay surfaces are explored, and are indeed part of the subject matter of their art. The variety of textures and surfaces present in their work is one of the markers of modern ceramics—a gauge of the distance come from the smooth porcelain surfaces dominant since the eighteenth century.

In traditional European sculpture the medium, marble or bronze, for example, is neither painted nor masked. In ceramics, however, the natural clay surface is usually covered by glaze, a melted glass that creates an impervious coat, enabling nonvitreous clay bodies to hold liquids and mimicking the coveted shiny smoothness of metal or glass. Its appearance in contemporary works of art with neither utilitarian nor social pretensions is important. A colored surface on a clay object can link the work with either the oldest ceramic traditions or the most innovative polychromed sculpture of the early twentieth century.

A glazed surface can be subservient to or perfectly integrated with the sculptural form of the piece: Walker's colors articulate the divisions of the vase and accentuate its volume by circling the vessel (see pl. 1); Price's colored planes define the sides and edges of his cups and assure their dominance over the variable and distorting effects of light and shadow (see cover and pl. 16). In contrast, the ceramic form can be subservient to its surface, as in the works of Rudy Autio and Siler. Further, the form and surface of the work may be in energetic conflict or tension, a condition apparent in the painted sculpture of Picasso and in the vessels of Woodman and Andrea Gill (see pls. 25 and 29).

Howard Kottler, Portrait of a Vase, *1979, paint on whiteware, 19" x 18" x 4", courtesy of the artist*
PLATE 26

In the works of Autio and Siler, where the painted surface is of primary interest, the silhouette of the vase is simple and loosely articulated, what ceramic historian Philip Rawson calls "baglike"(*Ceramics Monthly*, 1986). In *Hellgate Appaloosa* (pl. 28) the swirling horses and figure consume the vase. The handlelike projections that separate its front and back would be of minor significance to the vase's total shape if they did not have on their surface the dominating images of horse's head and woman's arching body. The figures seem to create the shape of the vessel.

Siler's cylindrical vase has two sides defined by distinct images (pl. 27). A running man races around the pot on one side. The angled line of his body pulls him swiftly against the vertical silhouette of the vase and the thick impasto of the white slip seems to speed him on his way. On the opposite ("flip") side of the pot is an image of stillness—the artist stands with poised brush contemplating a vase before him. It is a round vase with a running animal on its surface and it sits on a turntable like a rotating piano stool. The vase is about movement. It is a collection of objects and images that are round and that go around—vases, runners, turntables. We can imagine these figures on the rectangular canvases that Siler usually paints, but both the humor and the depth of this work stem from his use of a generic white cylindrical pot as his canvas.

Rudy Autio, Hellgate Appaloosa, *1984, glaze and slip on stoneware, 31" x 25" x 17", collection of SAFECO Insurance Companies*
PLATE 28

Patrick Siler, Putting on the Slip with Mr. Jiggy-Jaggy Man on the Flip Side, *1981, glaze and slip on stoneware, 12¾" x 7½" x 7½", Seattle Art Museum, purchased with funds from the Anne Gould Hauberg Craft Fund, 82.80*
PLATE 27

Andrea Gill, Undulating Winged Vessel, *1986, slip on earthenware, 27½″ x 17″ x 7″, courtesy of The Hand and the Spirit Gallery, Scottsdale, Arizona*
PLATE 29

In Kirk Mangus's *Another Blond* (pl. 30), the painted figure is at odds with the form of the pot. The artist creates a sharp contrast between two contours —the silhouette of the pot and the outline of the nude. The vessel's profile is a jagged ziggurat, with the steps roughly corresponding to the shoulder, waist, body, and foot of both the drawing and the vase. But the curvilinear nude is sliced by the geometric form and becomes fragmented and disjointed. The roughness of execution increases the tension and expressiveness of the piece and distances it from the elegant and smooth classical vases that are its predecessors.

It is also possible to read body imagery into Gill's *Undulating Winged Vessel* (pl. 29)— a long, elegant neck bifurcates the body of the pot into shoulder and breastlike forms. But there is no clear naturalistic imagery on the vessel. While Gill has made many pieces using explicit human figures, this work is self-referential—it is a painted vessel that poses questions about the relationship of surface to form, of inside to outside, and contour to edge. It is clearly related to early twentieth-century painted sculpture in both its mundane subject matter—the vase—and by its colorful, nondescriptive surface that interacts with the form (Elsen 1974, 102-9).

Kirk Mangus, Another Blond, *1984, slip on earthenware, 37″ x 10″ x 10″, courtesy of Dorothy Weiss Gallery, San Francisco*
PLATE 30

Gill's vessel has an interior, marked by the opening at the neck of the pot, and a silhouette, as do all dimensional works. But the winged flanges also have their own interior, unrelated to the inside of the vessel, and edges that are independent of the contour of the vase. These orange edges mark the thickness of the wings and are continued as painted lines on the surface of the pot. These painted lines are like pictures of an edge. Other linear reminders of the form of the vase are painted on its surface. Heart-shaped arcs begin at the top of the neck as simple lines mirroring both each other and the bulging body of the vessel. These arcs enclose space; they have an inside and an outside analogous to the vessel's interior and exterior. As the lines descend toward each other to form a point at the foot of the vessel, they define flat planes of pattern; they become edges analogous to the contour of a vase. Gill is showing us that both painting and sculpture can be enriched by association with each other.

FIGURE

Michael Lucero's dangling figure (pl. 31) has a vase head, like the cup-head in Shaw's *Cubist Coffee Cup* (see pl. 22). In both works, the artists retain a traditional vessel form as counterpoint to a daring and inventive use of the clay in the remainder of the figure. Lucero gives us skeleton and nerve ends—the inside rather than the skin of the body. He then denies the weight of the clay medium by suspending his construction and letting it turn in the air. This construction is unique and, except for the head, the opposite of the massive hollow format that we expect of a clay object. Lucero's vase is only one component of his figure, its head. For other artists, the vase becomes the figure itself.

The vase is associated with the human form through nomenclature of its parts (lip, shoulder, belly, foot) and through the symbolism of the female as a vessel—a negative space to the male's positive and a container for the fetus. In articulated vases, like those of Voulkos, Woodman, and Gill (see pls. 24, 25, and 29), the human form is a lingering presence, although no images are painted on the surface. The relative bilateral symmetry of these works suggests a figure that is still and upright, no matter how flamboyant the glazing or exaggerated the armlike handles.

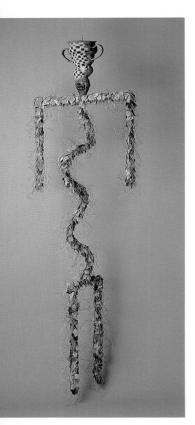

Michael Lucero, Untitled, *1981, slip and underglaze on stoneware and porcelain, wire, 96" x 36" x 36", collection of Linda Farris*
PLATE 31

The torsion of a moving body cannot be represented in a symmetrical form. As the vessel becomes more like a moving body, it becomes less like a vase. Thus the bent and twisted forms in Donna Polseno's and Arnold Zimmerman's vases approach the boundaries of figurative sculpture more closely than other works previously discussed (pls. 32 and 33). They emphatically remain vessels, however. This is because of the open and slightly flaring necks of the clay torsos, suggesting entry into the hollow interior. By creating vases as well as figures, Zimmerman and Polseno expand referents and meaning, absorbing the history of both sculpture and vessels into their work.

Donna Polseno, Untitled, 1984, glaze and slip on whiteware, 28" x 12" x 8", courtesy of the artist
PLATE 32

Arnold Zimmerman, Untitled,
*1985, stoneware, 109" x 39" x
39", courtesy of Objects
Gallery, Chicago*
PLATE 33

U ntil recently, students attracted to
the clay medium could count on
training in vesselmaking. The vocabulary of mud and wheel, inside
and out, function and surface, were universal to artists working in clay.
Painting students, de Kooning for example, drew the figure as part of
a classical education; ceramists made pots. De Kooning eventually discarded conventions of contour and proportion, but kept the figure as
an energetic, expressive element in his painting. Some potters too,
under many of the same influences, discarded the proportions, surfaces, and functions of the classical vessels they had learned to make.
But they kept the vessel as an idea or a formal boundary for at least
some of their work.

The retention of traditional forms, like the plate, the cup, and the
vase, links us to the shared history of all related images and to their
metaphorical associations. This is a reason why representational
images, no matter how distorted, will continue to occur in painting,
and that vessels, no matter how useless, will continue to be produced
in clay. We look at clay objects with eyes for form, line, and color, as
we look at any work of art. Adding knowledge of use, scale, touch,
form, and associations unique to the particular history of the medium,
we see an expansion, not a restriction, of possibilities.

CHECKLIST OF THE EXHIBITION
Dimensions are in inches.
Height precedes width and depth.

ROBERT ARNESON
American, b. 1930

1 *Dirty Dish*, 1971
Glaze and china paint on whiteware
8½ x 20½ x 8½
Seattle Art Museum, gift of the Sidney
and Anne Gerber Collection, 86.272
Plate 11

2 *Dirty Dish #14*, 1971
Glaze and china paint on whiteware
9 x 22 x 7
Collection of Sally Lilienthal

3 *Mountain Cup #18*, 1972
Glaze and slip on whiteware
4 x 5½ x 6¾
Collection of Robert Arneson and
Sandra Shannonhouse; courtesy of
Fuller Goldeen Gallery, San Francisco
Plate 14

4 *Sinking Cup*, 1974
Glazed whiteware
2½ x 14½ x 12
Collection of Mack L. Graham

5 *Describing the Diameter*, 1977
Glazed earthenware
18 x 18 x 2
Collection of Lynn Plotkin

6 *A Question of Measure with Colored
Grid*, 1980
Glaze, slip, china paint, and luster
on earthenware
18¾ x 18¾ x 2
Collection of Robert Arneson and
Sandra Shannonhouse
Plate 2

RUDY AUTIO
American, b. 1926

7 *Hellgate Appaloosa*, 1984
Glaze and slip on stoneware
31 x 25 x 17
Collection of SAFECO Insurance
Companies
Plate 28

8 *Santa Fe Soleares*, 1986
Glaze and slip on stoneware
29½ x 19½ x 18½
Courtesy of Traver Sutton Gallery,
Seattle

OLGA BRAVO
American, b. 1955

9 *Cup and Saucer*, 1985
Glaze, slip, and underglaze on
earthenware
11¾ x 12¼ x 2¾
Collection of Pamela and Stephen
Hootkin
Plate 21

10 *Cup*, 1986
Glaze, slip, and underglaze on
earthenware
24 x 13 x 4
Collection of Gene Lipitz

VIOLA FREY
American, b. 1933

11 *Horse and Face Plate*, 1978
Glazed whiteware
27 x 27 x 3
Courtesy of the artist and Rena Bransten
Gallery, San Francisco

12 *Untitled*, 1980
Glazed whiteware
25¼ x 25¼ x 2½
Collection of Mr. and Mrs. Earl Millard

13 *Winged Horse with Compartment*, 1986
Glazed whiteware
27 x 27 x 3
Courtesy of Rena Bransten Gallery,
San Francisco
Plate 5

ANDREA GILL
American, b. 1948

14 *Spiral Jar*, 1982
Slip on earthenware
23¼ x 11 x 11
Collection of Howard and Gwen Laurie
Smits

15 *Undulating Winged Vessel*, 1986
Slip on earthenware
27½ x 17 x 7
Courtesy of The Hand and the Spirit
Gallery, Scottsdale, Arizona
Plate 29

MARY HEILMANN
American, b. 1940

16 *Wall Drawing*, 1983
Acrylic on whiteware
12 x 12 x½
Courtesy of Pat Hearn Gallery, New York

17 *3-D Cup Drawing*, 1985
Oil on whiteware
8 x 20 x 6
Courtesy of Pat Hearn Gallery, New York
Plate 20

18 *4 Triangles*, 1985
Glazed whiteware
20 x 24 x 1
Courtesy of Pat Hearn Gallery, New York

TONY HEPBURN
American, born Great Britain, 1942

19 *Bottom*, 1979
Glazed stoneware and porcelain
6 x 18½ x 14
Collection of Ree Schonlau

20 *Cup Slide*, 1979
Glazed stoneware and porcelain
7 x 24 x 13
Collection of Laura Hepburn
Plate 17

JUN KANEKO
Japanese (living in the U.S.), b. 1942

21 *Untitled Plate #403*, 1987
Glaze and slip on stoneware
25 x 21 x 2½
Courtesy of Klein Gallery, Chicago
Plate 7

22 *Untitled Plate #401*, 1987
Glaze and slip on stoneware
25 x 21 x 2½
Courtesy of Klein Gallery, Chicago

HOWARD KOTTLER
American, b. 1930

23 *Cup of Lite*, 1973
Whiteware
5 x 7 x 3
Courtesy of the artist
Plate 19

24 *Homage to Oppenheim*, 1973
Fur and paint on whiteware
5 x 7 x 3
Courtesy of the artist

25 *Paisley Cup*, 1973
Glaze and decals on whiteware
4½ x 6½ x 4½
Courtesy of the artist

26 *Portrait of a Vase*, 1979
Paint on whiteware
19 x 18 x 4
Courtesy of the artist
Plate 26

27 *Wood Vase*, 1979
Contac paper on whiteware
16½ x 11½ x 3¾
Courtesy of the artist

MICHAEL LUCERO
American, b. 1953

28 *Untitled*, 1981
Slip and underglaze on stoneware and
porcelain; wire
96 x 36 x 36
Collection of Linda Farris
Plate 31

KIRK MANGUS
American, b. 1952

29 *Another Blond*, 1984
Slip on earthenware
37 x 10 x 10
Courtesy of Dorothy Weiss Gallery,
San Francisco
Plate 30

30 *Girl With Ponytail*, 1984
Slip on earthenware
33½ x 12 x 9½
Collection of Mr. and Mrs. Earl Millard

MICHAEL MORAN
American, b. 1942

31 *Untitled*, 1984
Glazed earthenware
20 x 20¼ x 3¾
Collection of Jano Moran

32 *Woman on a Black Horse*, 1986
Glaze, slip, and miscellaneous fired
materials on stoneware
21 x 21 x 2½
Seattle Art Museum, purchased with
funds from the Anne Gould Hauberg
Craft Fund, 87.12
Plate 8

RON NAGLE
American, b. 1939

33 *Stuccoyama No. 1*, 1978
Glaze and china paint on whiteware
4¼ x 4¾ x 4½
Collection of Mr. and Mrs. Earl Millard

34 *Cup*, 1980
Glaze and china paint on whiteware
5 x 4¾ x 4¾
Collection of Museum of Art, Rhode
Island School of Design, Providence,
Marken Scholes Shedd Memorial Fund,
81.062

35 *Untitled VI/7.2.82*, 1982
Glaze and china paint on whiteware
6½ x 3¾ x 3¾
Collection of Mr. and Mrs. William L.
Nussbaum
Plate 15

DONNA POLSENO
American, b. 1950

36 *Untitled*, 1984
Glaze and slip on whiteware
28 x 12 x 8
Courtesy of the artist
Plate 32

37 *Untitled*, 1984
Glaze and slip on whiteware
34 x 11 x 7
Courtesy of the artist

KENNETH PRICE
American, b. 1935

38 *Slate Cup*, 1972
Acrylic on whiteware
5½ x 6 x 5
Collection of Edwin Janss
Plate 16

39 *Architectural Cup*, 1973
Glazed whiteware
4½ x 4 x 3¼
Collection of Edwin Janss

40 *Untitled Cup #8*, 1973-74
Glazed whiteware
3 x 4 x 4 (cup); ½ x 2½ x 1 (bar)
Seattle Art Museum, Contemporary Art
Acquisition Fund, 79.32
Cover

41 *Wave*, 1980
Glazed whiteware
5½ x 9½ x 5½
Courtesy of Charles Cowles Gallery,
New York

TOM RIPPON
American, b. 1954

42 *Miss-Stress #1*, 1986
Glaze, luster, and acrylic on porcelain
8 x 6 x 6 (overall)
Courtesy of the artist
Plate 23

43 *Miss-Stress #2*, 1986
Glaze, luster, and acrylic on porcelain
5 x 4¾ x 4¾ (overall)
Courtesy of the artist

44 *Miss-Stress #3*, 1986
Glaze, luster, and acrylic on porcelain
4 x 3½ x 3½ (overall)
Courtesy of the artist

RICHARD SHAW
American, b. 1941

45 *Confetti Twig Cup*, 1972
Glazed porcelain
7¼ x 6 x 6
Collection of Martha Shaw

46 *House of Cards with Torn King*, 1976
Glaze, decals, and luster on porcelain
7½ x 6¾ x 6¾
Collection of Diana Fuller

47 *Cubist Coffee Cup*, 1985
Glaze and decals on porcelain
30¼ x 11½ x 16
Collection of Mr. and Mrs. John B.
Stuppin
Plate 22

48 *Untitled plate (1 B)*, 1986
Glaze and decals on porcelain
20¼ x 20¼ x 1½
Courtesy of Braunstein/Quay Gallery,
San Francisco

49 *Untitled (25 B)*, 1986
Glaze and decals on porcelain
20 x 20 x 1¾
Courtesy of Braunstein/Quay Gallery,
San Francisco
Plate 12

PETER SHIRE
American, b. 1947

50 *Checkered Peach Cup*, 1977-78
Colored earthenware
4 x 8 x 3¼
Collection of the artist
Plate 13

51 *Smile Cup*, 1977-78
Glaze on colored earthenware
5½ x 7 x 7
Collection of the artist

PATRICK SILER
American, b. 1939

52 *Bow-wow*, 1975
Glazed stoneware
14½ x 14½ x 1¼
Courtesy of the artist and Linda Farris
Gallery, Seattle
Plate 3

53 *Shoe*, 1977
Glaze and slip on stoneware
16 x 16 x 1½
Courtesy of the artist and Linda Farris
Gallery, Seattle

54 *Putting on the Slip with Mr. Jiggy-Jaggy Man on the Flip Side*, 1981
Glaze and slip on stoneware
12¾ x 7½ x 7½
Seattle Art Museum, purchased with
funds from the Anne Gould Hauberg
Craft Fund, 82.80
Plate 27

55 *Black Rabbit Vase*, 1985
Glaze and slip on stoneware
12 x 9 x 9
Courtesy of the artist and Linda Farris
Gallery, Seattle

ROBERT SPERRY
American, b. 1927

56 *Untitled #724*, 1986
Slip on stoneware
28½ x 28½ x 4½
Courtesy of the artist

57 *Untitled #735*, 1986
Slip on stoneware
28½ x 28½ x 4½
Courtesy of the artist
Cover and Plate 4

IRVIN TEPPER
American, b. 1947

58 *Decaf Morning*, 1985
Porcelain
9½ x 10¾ x 14
Courtesy of Gallery Paule Anglim,
San Francisco

59 *Bright Ideas*, 1986
Porcelain
9¾ x 10 x 14
Courtesy of Gallery Paule Anglim,
San Francisco
Plate 18

PETER VOULKOS
American, b. 1924

60 *Ceramic Drawing #12*, 1977
Stoneware
22 x 22 x 4¼
Seattle Art Museum, Margaret E. Fuller
Purchase Fund, 78.66

61 *Goshun*, 1980
Stoneware
47¾ x 18 x 18
Collection of Lynn Plotkin

62 *Untitled*, 1982
Stoneware
42 x 28 x 28
Collection of Mr. and Mrs. William L.
Nussbaum
Plate 24

63 *Untitled (RB 11)*, 1982
Stoneware
22 x 22 x 5½
Courtesy of Braunstein/Quay Gallery,
San Francisco and Images Gallery,
Sun Valley, Idaho
Plate 10

JAMIE WALKER
American, b. 1958

64 *Untitled*, 1985
Glaze, slip, and glass on porcelain
22 x 20 x 20
Courtesy of Traver Sutton Gallery, Seattle
Cover and Plate 1

65 *Column*, 1986
Glaze and slip on stoneware and
porcelain
85½ x 21 x 21
Courtesy of Dorothy Weiss Gallery,
San Francisco

66 *Hideaway*, 1986
Glaze and slip on porcelain
23 x 17 x 3
Collection of Mr. and Mrs. Mayer Shacter

67 *Double Spiral*, 1986
Glaze and slip on porcelain
23 x 17 x 3
Courtesy of Dorothy Weiss Gallery,
San Francisco
Plate 6

STAN WELSH
American, b. 1951

68 *Mind Puzzle*, 1986
Glazed earthenware
24 x 26 x 4½
Courtesy of Dorothy Weiss Gallery,
San Francisco
Plate 9

69 *Reflector*, 1986
Glazed earthenware
24 x 24 x 3½
Courtesy of Dorothy Weiss Gallery,
San Francisco

BETTY WOODMAN
American, b. 1930

70 *Sunrise Vase and Shadow*, 1985
Glazed earthenware
26 x 29 x 12 (vase); 26 x 29 x 1½
(shadow)
Courtesy of Greenberg Gallery, St. Louis

71 *Sturdy Vase and Shadow*, 1985
Glazed earthenware
22½ x 19 x 9 (vase); 22 x 21 x 1½
(shadow)
Courtesy of Greenberg Gallery, St. Louis
Plate 25

ARNOLD ZIMMERMAN
American, b. 1954

72 *Untitled*, 1985
Stoneware
109 x 39 x 39
Courtesy of Objects Gallery, Chicago
Plate 33

73 *Untitled*, 1985
Stoneware
108 x 46 x 46
Courtesy of Objects Gallery, Chicago

Because many terms relating to clay have
various definitions, the following is offered
for use in this catalogue.

PORCELAIN: fine-grained, vitreous, high-fire
(usually above 2000° F), white clay.

STONEWARE: coarsely-grained, vitreous,
high-fire, off-white to brown clay.

EARTHENWARE: low-fire red or brown clay.

WHITEWARE: low-fire white clay.

GLAZE: fired coating containing glass-
forming substances; used to make clay
impervious to liquids, to create a smooth
or textured surface, and/or to color a
ceramic object.

SLIP, UNDERGLAZE, CHINA PAINT, AND LUSTERS:
fired coatings containing little or no glass-
forming chemicals; used to texture and/or
color the clay surface.

SELECTED BIBLIOGRAPHY

Benezra, Neal. *Robert Arneson: A Retrospective.* Des Moines, Iowa: Des Moines Art Center, 1985.

Clark, Garth, ed. *Ceramic Art, Comment and Review 1882-1977.* New York: E. P. Dutton, 1978.

Clark, Garth. *A Century of Ceramics in the United States, 1878-1978.* New York: E. P. Dutton, 1979.

Dormer, Peter. *The New Ceramics, Trends and Traditions.* London: Thames and Hudson Ltd., 1986.

Elsen, Albert E. *Origins of Modern Sculpture: Pioneers and Premises.* New York: George Braziller, Inc., 1974.

Harrington, LaMar. *Ceramics in the Pacific Northwest: A History.* Seattle: University of Washington Press, 1979.

Lucie-Smith, Edward. *The Story of Craft, the Craftsman's Role in Society.* Ithaca, N. Y. and Oxford: Cornell University and Phaidon Press Ltd., 1981.

Perrone, Jeff. *The Ceramics of Betty Woodman.* Reading, Pa.: Albright College, 1985.

_____. "More Sherds." *American Ceramics* 4 (1986): 24-37.

Rawson, Philip. *Ceramics.* Philadelphia: University of Pennsylvania Press, 1984. (First published Oxford University Press, 1971.)

_____. "Vessel as Center." *American Ceramics* 4 (1985): 28-31.

_____. "Empty Vessels." *Ceramics Monthly* (September 1986): 55-57.

Slivka, Rose. "The New Ceramic Presence." *Craft Horizons* 21 (1961): 30-37.

_____. *Peter Voulkos.* New York: New York Graphic Society, 1978.

Wechsler, Susan. *Low Fire Ceramics.* New York: Watson-Guptill Publications, 1981.

Woodman, George. "Ceramic Decoration and the Concept of Ceramics as a Decorative Art." *American Ceramics* 1 (1982): 30-33.

INDEX OF ARTISTS
All references are to page numbers;
text references appear in roman type,
illustrations in *italic*.